Motherfield

JULIA CIMAFIEJEVA

MOTHERFIELD

poems and protest diary

translated from Belarusian by
Valzhyna Mort and Hanif Abdurraqib

PHONEME
MEDIA

DEEP
VELLUM

DALLAS, TEXAS

Phoneme Media, an imprint of Deep Vellum
3000 Commerce St., Dallas, Texas 75226
deepvellum.org · @deepvellum

Deep Vellum Publishing
3000 Commerce St., Dallas, Texas 75226
deepvellum.org · @deepvellum

Deep Vellum is a 501c3 nonprofit literary arts organization
founded in 2013 with the mission to bring
the world into conversation through literature.

FIRST PRINTING

ISBN: 978-1-64605-225-7 (paperback)
ISBN: 978-1-64605-251-6 (eBook)

LIBRARY OF CONGRESS CONTROL NUMBER: 2022941372

Cover design by In-House International Creative
Interior layout & typesetting by KGT

PRINTED IN THE UNITED STATES OF AMERICA

CONTENTS

from *The Protest Diary*

August 2020–March 2021*

* The text, originally written in English, has been edited by the translators.

August 7, two days until the election:

Waiting for you, I find a nice bench in Yanka Kupala Park, close to Niezaliežnasci Avenue, open my notebook, and start musing. People pass by, I notice the white bracelets on their arms, a sign of their vote for change. Not taking my eyes from the page, I follow a conversation between a man and a woman who are arguing. He wants to show a victory sign to the cyclists riding in dozens along the central streets. A lot of them wear bracelets or ribbons, some are even holding flags. These innocent signs make it easy for police to spot them in the crowd. So the woman is not happy about her man's desire to show solidarity. He could be detained.

The sky is navy blue when we cross Yakub Kolas Square. It is warm and calm under the old birches that grow next to the bronze sculpture of a boy playing a flute. Groups of cyclists swiftly move by on both sides of the square. Suddenly we notice a pair of OMON officers dressed in black, their faces totally covered but for two narrow slits for their pupils to scrutinize the world. They look like aliens on the Minsk summer streets, patrolling the occupied territory. I spit with disgust in their direction. We are too far for them to notice. Then, near the Philharmonic Hall, on the opposite side of the road, a prison van stops, soldiers in olive-colored uniforms jump out of it and run. With others, we pause to watch. When they drag a young man in a white T-shirt into the van, I start filming. People cry: "Fascists! Fascists!" I'd like to join this angry choir, but you ask me to go home.

Two days ago, I wrote "My European Poem."

August 8, one day until the election:

Our friends Ihar and Ania suggest having a little outing somewhere: in a quiet picturesque place near Drazdy Lake or the so-called Minsk Sea. I am too restless, I can't work, scrolling the Facebook timeline and the Telegram feed. Multiple cases of falsifications at the polling stations, detentions of independent observers. My Ukrainian translator, Ia, has messaged about one of my poems and while we are discussing the Ukrainian translation of "My Motherland," you prepare a dough in the kitchen. During the dull pandemic times in the early spring, making bread became your passion.

We are lying on the shore, looking at the sun reflecting in the tiny waves of the artificial Belarusian sea, eating (your bread receives lots of praise!), drinking, speaking about politics and our future. Ania, having brought her suit, can't miss the opportunity to go swimming. I remember how several years ago we were in the writer's residency at Wannsee Lake near Berlin. I remember those black-and-white photos from the old times hanging on the stands. Maybe in the late 1930s people were bathing there with the same carelessness? Or am I exaggerating as I lie on the blanket of needles under the high pines?

August 9, election day:

My polling station is in a three-story school building. There is a huge, asphalted yard in front of it, dull-looking flower beds, and all the property is surrounded by a green barred metal fence. An ordinary city school. Just outside of the fence, under the tree shade, four people with paper sheets in their hands stand peering keenly through the fence. Their backpacks and bottles of water are by their side on the ground. These are the independent election observers who are not allowed to be present even on the premises of the school, they have to "observe" from a fifty-meter distance.

Every election day in Lukashenka's Belarus has turned into a demonstration of the cheap and vulgar aesthetics of his power. The school entrance is decorated with red, white, and green balloon garlands. By the front stairs, there is a big Alivaria Beer tent where two festively dressed saleswomen sell beer, vodka, juice, chips, sausages, bread, and sandwiches with onion and herring. At the tables near the tent some of the voters are celebrating their freedom to vote.

Loud pop music is another attribute of Lukashenka's election culture. A teenage girl in a pseudo-folk costume with a wreath on her head is singing about her love for the Motherland, passionately clenching a microphone. Her Russian song checks off the golden wheat fields, the big blue lakes, and the slender white storks flying over our heads. She sings that we all live safely and peacefully in our beloved Belarus.

I pass my passport to a mustached election committee member. In his short-sleeved shirt, he could be a shop teacher or a supply manager. When he passes me a ballot, my hands are shaking: before throwing the ballot into the ballot box, I have to check it for any markings. Committee members are known to put dots on the ballots so that later they can invalidate them as wrongly filled out. Also, I take a photo of mine so that my vote is counted on a special online platform. All these actions could irritate the mustached man, but he stays cool.

Now your brother Illya is driving us to Šabany, the non-prestigious residential neighborhood in the southeast of Minsk where you both grew up, where your parents still live. The polling station is situated in the much-hated former school you once left. Eight years ago, when living in exile in Hamburg, you wrote a novel about your neighborhood, *Šabany: The Story of One Disappearance*, about the impossibility of return: "Šabany is not a village. Neither is it a city. Šabany is like that amateur guitar song that is neither true music nor true poetry, it is an established oddity, an officially acknowledged nonexistence, the eternally new clothes of the long-dead emperor."

After a little feast of a squash salad and champagne toasts to our future victory at your parents' apartment, your sister-in-law drives us home. The internet is already switched off in the whole country. We can read neither news websites nor Facebook.

In the evening we return to my polling station to see the results in person. The place looks different in the fresh dusk of the night. About a hundred people are waiting there. Suddenly, two headlights beam through the side street. A small police car approaches the school gate. A pair of policemen watches us. We all get stiff; we watch them back with dark excitement. In a minute the car turns round and drives away. Then it returns followed by a yellow bus with dark windows. We stiffen again, the bus might be filled with policemen. But as it comes closer, we breathe out. Teachers who have served on the election committee start hurriedly climbing into the inner darkness of the bus. Without announcing the results of the count, one by one, with their heads shrunk into their shoulders, they board. We start shouting: "Shame! Cowards!"

The Telegram app works when I use it through multiple proxy servers. There, I read that military vehicles are heading for the city center. Lydia Jarmošyna, the eternal Central Committee chairperson, has called the long voting lines "provocation and sabotage." Brief reports from the streets of Minsk, from big and small towns around the country, come at every moment. The reports describe police violence, military vehicles driving into peaceful gatherings, stun grenades thrown at the unarmed, shooting at the peaceful protesters who disagree with the results of the rigged election. I feel nailed down to the kitchen stool. Despite the proxy servers, the internet connection is nasty. Dozens of pictures and videos are loading slowly and, once loaded, are horrible to see. Through the open window we hear the terrifying sounds of the war, we see the bright sparks of the blasts.

August 10, second day of protests:

"Is it blood?" I ask you as I study a range of round brown stains on the pavement. They do look like dried drops. I take photos of the stains, I want them to be kept, to be remembered. It's noon now. The air is hot and humid. The shadow of my head is touching the dried blood splatter.

Xi Jinping, Kassym-Jomart Tokayev, and Vladimir Putin congratulated Lukashenka on his victory. But I feel as if election night has not ended yet, as if we are still living through the same long election day. I feel nausea.

The closer we come to the Pushkin metro station, the more people we see around. Several thousands of them are standing at the four corners of the capacious intersection of Pushkin Avenue and Prytycki Street. On the roadside we stand chanting "Žyvie Belarus!" ("Viva Belarus!") and "Uhadzi!" ("Go away!"), we clap our hands, we smile to each other. No leader will come, we know, no speech will be made. We should organize ourselves; we should show that we resist.

No police personnel or military vehicles are in sight, just cars honking and people clapping. Though somebody says that on Kalvaryjskaja Street, not far from here, they have already started to disperse people. But we are free at this moment, like children left alone at home.

The number of people is growing every minute. On the opposite side of the street, on the hill by Aurora Cinema, there are several thousand people, someone is waving a big white-red-white flag. Suddenly the protesters start descending onto the roadway, blocking traffic, and leaving only one lane out of three for transport. It's getting darker, the air is electrified, and observing people put big flowerpots on the road to build a barricade, you suggest that the police must be on the way by now, so we better leave.

12

It's half past nine, it's twilight. By now the courtyards could be full of riot police ambushing those who, like us, decide to leave the peaceful gathering early. We pass people waving by the roadside, cars stuck in the traffic jam with their doors ajar and music playing loud, bikers dressed in leather talking and laughing. In a shop close to our building, we buy a beer for me and cheap wine for you, our unhealthy ritual.

Already on the stairs, while you are opening the door and talking to the cat meeting us irritably, I start reading the news. Protests are happening everywhere in Minsk: Hrušauka, Malinauka, Sierabranka, Uručča, by the Michalova metro station, and near Riga shopping mall. There are actions in other cities and towns: Mahiliou, Mazyr, Hrodna, Barysau, Homiel, Viciebsk, Berascie, Mar'ina Horka, Kobryn, Smarhon', Žabinka. Predictably, the protesters are met with the same brutality of the previous night: stun grenades, rubber bullets, beatings, and detentions. A *Nasha Niva* newspaper journalist has been purposely shot in her leg. A bus driver has been seriously injured. A lot of people have been wounded by grenades thrown into gatherings.

We drink beer and wine; we open the window to hear the blasts and the nonstop honking of the cars blocking Pushkin Avenue. At 23:46 I read that a person has been killed on Prytycki Street. All night we sit in our tiny kitchen, listening to the blasts in the darkness behind the windows. We stay up late. Election day has not yet ended.

August 11, one day after the first murder:

Big plastic vases stand empty by the underground flower shops. With their arms crossed, the saleswomen talk to each other in low voices looking suspiciously at the passersby. One saleswoman has four long stems of yellow flowers for us, with water dripping from their sharp ends onto the concrete floor. "Your price seems too high," I foolishly say to her. Now she is upset, she is not "exploiting the situation." I get ashamed, I haven't bought flowers for so long, it's kind of a luxury. We bring them to the spot where last night a man was killed, and we stand still along with others. Hills of flowers rise on all four corners of the intersection and there's also a big bunch in the center of the crossing. I observe a car passenger stretch an arm out of the window and throw red and white roses on the road.

Under the glaring sun we walk across the bridge toward the industrial district along Kazlova Street. The workers at the Minsk Electrotechnical Plant are supposedly on strike, we want to check whether it's true and maybe support them somehow. There have not been any strikes in Belarus since the 1990s. The workers then had mostly economic claims, today they are protesting the rigged election, the police brutality, the detentions, and the internet shutdown. By the entrance, around ten people talk and laugh, mostly youngsters. They look more like university students on a summer break than working-class people. No more workers have come out of the building to support them. So is there any sense in standing here then?

We meet L. by the seafood store Ocean, and she tells us that martial law will be imposed soon. The shops will be closed, people won't be allowed to leave their homes. That's how they plan to stop the protests. Today at 18:00, the internet will be switched off, officially. "Something needs to be done," L. says. "To spread information, we should make leaflets and put them into the postboxes in our apartment blocks." In the block where you and I live now, there is only one postbox, big, white, with the number 61, a double-headed eagle, and the heading: RUSSIA. The mail received by the rest of the residents is stacked on the windowsill and spread on the dusty radiator on the ground floor.

My phone starts ringing, it's Ania. People are being packed by the police into prison vans by the Electrotechnical Plant. We were lucky to leave early.

August 12:

Today we have the internet back. And while reading the Facebook posts of my friends who finally have an opportunity to share their experience, I feel like I'm reading a book that might be written by Ales Adamovič or Sviatlana Alexievič. The same polyphonic choir that made me cry as a teenager over the book *Out of the Fire* (I also cried while reading *Voices from Chernobyl* and it was sobbing that prevented me from finishing *Secondhand Time*). Maybe later some author will compile all these painful posts and commentaries into one book, a document of the time that will tell what we have felt these days.

I can't build barricades, I can't run fast, I can't fight against the armed police. I join a women's protest near the Kamarouka market. With flowers in their hands, they wave at the passing cars that honk back, even though a driver could be detained for honking. In my bag I have packed a small kit in case of detention. When the women hear that prison vans are lining up a few blocks ahead, most of them stay. "The police will not be able to imprison us all," the girls say.

August 15:

Today Aliaksandr Taraykouski was buried. We come to the Pushkin metro station, where he was killed by the police. A memorial has been improvised here with flowers stuck into the fence, placards that read "You should be alive," flags, ribbons, and balloons. We mourn his death and the death of another Aliaksandr who was tortured by the police in the city of Homiel. At the same time, it is exciting to be here on the sunlit hills of Pushkin Avenue together with others. It's hard for me to admit, but I feel like their deaths are sacrifices for our freedom. Would these deaths suffice for the dictator and his accomplices to go away, or will there be more?

Ihar and Ania take us by car to the exhibit "The Art of the Regime" in front of the Palace of Arts on Kazlova Street. A dozen artists stand holding photos of people tortured in the detention centers. Faces caked with blood, blue and red bruises on legs and arms, plastered limbs, bandaged heads, swollen eyes full of terror. The cars honk and cheer.

August 16:

Today the biggest protest in the history of Belarus takes place. It's unbelievable how many people are here! How many do not want to tolerate the inhumanity of the state, how many are ready for changes. We are smiling to people around us, to each other. When was the last time I was so happy? Maybe when we started dating?

No program is planned, no leaders are to have their speeches in front of the hundreds of thousands of people. No, we are here on our own. We walk, we chant, we take selfies. The strangest thing is there is no police, as if they were hiding, waiting, or as if they did not exist at all. "The city is ours!" we cry. From Niezaliežnasci Square we walk home on foot.

In the evening, lying on the sofa with aching legs and a throat sore from chanting, I feel the surreal nature of what has been happening. All those people on both sides of Peramožcau Avenue, on the green lawns—it's forbidden to step or sit there, though no one knows why. All those hundreds of small and huge flags flying, even the statue of the Mother Homeland, a sacred symbol of the Belarusian regime, covered with the white-red-white flag. Maria Kalesnikava on the steps of the KGB building demanding that all the political prisoners be released immediately.

October 1:

I feel safe inside the body of a crowd. I've never heard of any cases of pick-pocketing or violence between the demonstrators. People distribute bottles of water and food. You can easily be caught by policemen on your way to the rally or after it, when the protest body is weak. But inside of it, the masked men won't touch us.

Back in August, in the first days after the election, people walked freely in the streets with flags on their shoulders or held high over their heads. Then the government decided to get rid of the surplus of democracy.

Every Sunday starts with the news that dozens of military trucks full of riot police, water cannons, and special assault barrage complexes are heading for the city from the suburbs. Soviet monuments and main squares are defended by soldiers and encircled with barbed wire. Central shopping malls and metro stations are closed for "security reasons," streets are cordoned off, public transport stopped. The internet is switched off every Sunday.

We leave prepared for the worst. First, I dress carefully, in case I end up spending a night or two in the detention center. Second, I intensively water my dozens of flowerpots. Third, we leave our cat enough food for a few days. One of my friends says that her cat has become fat with all these Sunday rallies. Fourth, we take passports and a bottle of water. It's important to clear all the history off your cell phone: police check your conversations and social media for "antigovernmental" opinions.

When Alexander Lukashenka came to power in 1994, I was twelve years old and lived with my family in a village in the southeast of Belarus. My parents were among those who voted for him then; most of the village-dwellers did, he appeared to be one of them, a collective farm chairman.

As a child I was fascinated by Lukashenka's charisma—on television, speaking to ministers and other officials, he looked so sure of himself, so firm and harsh. My younger sister and I spent hours in front of the TV listening to his public admonishing of officials.

I went to my first opposition demonstration in 2000, not long after I started living as a student in Minsk.

Prior to this August's election, I felt scared about the unpredictability of the events to come. I wanted to write a poem, but I couldn't find the words in Belarusian. So, I wrote my first poem in English, "My European Poem." I tried to express my fear and to find in a foreign language the hope I lacked in my own.

When I wrote that poem, I was afraid at the thought that I might be detained by the riot police. Now, with the daily detention of my friends—journalists, photographers, poets, dancers, scholars, teachers, doctors, historians, artists, many of the smartest people I know—I have gotten used to the idea.

Sometimes I feel ashamed that I've never been in a prison van. My only experience has been running away from the balaclava-wearing police when we arrived at a meeting spot too early. There were just a thousand people on both sides of Niezaliežnasci Avenue then. We all were waiting for the others to come when suddenly five olive prison vans, followed by several minibuses, appeared in a line, blocking those across the street. OMON started pulling people out of the human chain.

The protesters on our side of the street were shouting: "Fascists! Fascists!" The prison vans turned in our direction and we ran like children through the inner yards of the old buildings and managed to escape into a huge stream of people.

When they take away your vote, use your voice. This is the main instrument of our protest. It's not only about chanting at the demonstrations. A poem read aloud and a song sung in the public space become the weapons of the revolution.

A friend of mine, the poet and musician Uladz, was detained in September during a protest over the arrest of opposition leader Maria

Kalesnikava. There is a famous photo taken some minutes before his arrest: he and other men are being shielded by rows of women, both frightened and fierce, as a militiaman looks on. Together, they sang the mournful folk song "Kupalinka."

At his court hearing three days later, Uladz was asked about the purpose of his singing. He answered: "Because when you sing, you are not afraid." He was sentenced to six days in jail.

Just after the elections, a choir—that later named themselves the Free Choir—came out to the steps of the Belarusian State Philharmonic in Minsk and sang folk songs and old patriotic tunes to show their opposition to the government's violence. On one of those days, I was invited to read my poem "The Stone of Fear" in front of the choir. No microphone, just my voice, addressed to the people. I managed to finish the reading, but during the song that came after—"Mighty God," an unofficial Belarusian anthem—the police stepped in to disperse the crowd. The singers started slowly leaving the steps of the Philharmonic Hall but did not stop singing the hymn until the end.

When it became too unsafe to gather by the hall, the choir started singing in different public spaces: in shopping malls, the railway station, the subway. The gathering place is not revealed in advance. Two songs—and they are gone. "Be like water" is another slogan of our protests, the same as the one used by Hong Kong protesters.

The authorities try to threaten us with their military vehicles and their brutality, but we see that it is they who are most afraid. They are afraid of the flags in the windows of the apartment blocks, of the white-red-white ribbons and graffiti. Policemen are sent to take them down. They are afraid of songs; they are afraid of smiles. When citizens throw parties with their neighbors, riot police are sent to disperse them. They are afraid of theater. The Yanka Kupala National Theatre, the oldest in Belarus, was closed and its director fired when he condemned the violence committed by the state. Most of the actors resigned in solidarity with him.

October 4, fifty-seventh day of protests:

If we are going, then it's high time to get ready. Internet on our cell phones is already switched off, central metro stations closed. The Minsk Hero City Obelisk, Stela—where the demonstrations usually start—is the holy sanctuary of the regime. The memorial is dedicated to the victory of the Soviet people in WWII. Today, as every Sunday since August, it is traditionally decorated with barbed wire. Against the background of the tall monument, the lonely figures of military personnel look like a human garland hung by a crazy hand.

In summer, the colors of the walkouts were white and red. October weather changed the palette. The colors have darkened, spotted with bright umbrellas and colorful jackets.

Today's manifestation is called The Rally for the Release of Political Prisoners. There are seventy-four of them in jail now. Between August and the end of September, more than twelve thousand people have been kidnapped and beaten by police. Our crowd heads toward Akrescina, an infamous detention center in the west of Minsk. During the three August nights following the elections, its yard and cells became torture chambers. Thousands of people were savagely beaten there.

The level of brutality was a shock to everybody. It was revealed when the first people were released from Akrescina and other detention centers around Belarus. We saw broken arms and legs, blood-covered faces, terrible bruises covering bodies. We heard horrible stories full of anguish and dread. I could not discuss this with anybody; the words failed me. Could a human being do that to another human being for no reason at all, here in Belarus, where we have been reading stories of Nazi tortures since childhood? Not a single policeman has been punished for what was done, not a single criminal case opened. On the contrary, the victims who try to open a case against their torturers get prosecuted for daring to seek justice. Anybody can be accused of taking part in an unauthorized event and given a sentence.

But here we are on Pushkin Avenue, walking in the road and shouting: "Freedom to political prisoners!" and "Look out of the window and not into the TV screen" (in Russian it sounds shorter). Run-down dorms for factory workers stand on both sides of the avenue. It's Sunday, most of them are at home, smoking on wide balconies with colorful laundry drying behind men's bare torsos. They look at the people marching on the road. Never before have they seen a march of a hundred thousand so close. Dorm residents are showing victory signs to the protesters and cheering them on. "Join us! Join us!" the demonstrators shout.

I think about your headache and joint pain, though you believe that I have forgotten. I feel guilty and look at you, trying to understand if you feel better. By your reactions I see that you do. Meanwhile, we approach Akrescina detention center. By the tall poplar trees, I look back and see that the number of people behind us is dwindling. Where are those thousands of people? We halt on the grass a dozen meters before a white wall that wraps around the ugly palace of pain and grief. I hope that one day Akrescina will turn into a museum of Lukashenka's reign so that people do not forget what can happen if one agrees to tolerate a dictator.

We notice that the volunteer camp that has been standing here since the first protest days is empty. There is no one in the tents where the released could get medical, psychological, and legal help, could eat, drink, cry, and pray, could make a telephone call and get a ride home for free. Volunteers used to ask people not to make a lot of noise because the torturers were only more vicious when they heard the voices from outside. I guess the torturers wanted to make sure that they heard only the screams of their victims.

The most important skill of a Belarusian protester is to come to and leave the demonstration without being detained. Behind the trees I notice an ambulance car parked by the grocery shop and a policeman dressed like an astronaut by its side. Ambulance cars are often used by the police to stay unnoticed. We should always pay attention to the driver: if he wears a black balaclava, the "doctors" inside are not going to relieve your pain but inflict it.

At home we exhale and hug. Another protest Sunday is over, and we are still free.

October 11:

We have to be on alert all the time. We have already been running today with others on the wet grass and muddy tracks in the old central neighborhood. It felt like a cheap horror movie or a bad dream. Now we are hiding in a big mall, Corona. Under the dazzling lights of the shopping center I recover my breath and phone my brother to learn the news. While calling I look at the bright and colorful advertisements with huge half-naked women, relaxed and smiling. Their gazes invite us to stay in this gleaming, dry, and safe paradise, to smell perfumes, to order pizza, or at least to dry off. But we uninterestedly walk through the mall to the door on the opposite side and find ourselves in front of the immense demonstration marching along.

We are walking in the roadway on Pushkin Avenue when I begin to sense something sinister in the air. We've marched enough, you are sick, we've gotten soaked through, maybe it's time to go home? We climb over the metal fence that divides the road into two lanes. It's quite low, you just have to lift your leg, but your jeans are too tight, you could tear them. Crossing the lane, I suddenly look back and see that the demonstrators are running from the roadway into the courtyards. We run and everybody around us runs: young and old, women and men, workers and students, doctors and programmers. It doesn't matter who you are, the most important thing is how fast you can run from the police, across the playgrounds, across the parking lots, between the apartment blocks with their doorways opened by compassionate dwellers who invite strangers inside their flats. Even a small apartment can become a shelter for up to thirty people. It reminds me of the WWII stories about saving Jews. But you and I don't need to hide and find shelter now, we need to get home.

When it seems that the danger is over and at last we can catch our breath, behind the trees we notice another group of the protesters running toward us, and we start running again. Suddenly you stop. You cannot run anymore. We have to hide somewhere, and you suggest a grocery store. We enter quickly, take a shopping basket, and stop in the bread section as if we were normal customers. It is clear that we are not. We are soaking wet, water dripping from our hair, our faces red from running, our eyes the wild eyes of animals. We are trying to regulate our breathing over the bread loaves.

I dry my face and hair with a paper napkin; bending over the refrigerator full of dumplings, I try to calm down. There are no more police in sight, just customers wandering among the food shelves or demonstrators pretending to be customers, who knows. Finally, holding a shopping basket with wine and food for dinner, we go to the cashier. I have my backpack on and we usually try to be ecological, refusing the plastic bag, but not this time. This time we need an alibi.

Through the store windows we see that people are still marching. The store manager has already closed the door and is shouting at anyone twitching the handle from the outside. "Go away!" she cries at them, and "We are closed!" She lets us out and closes the glass door behind our backs.

Heading home you suggest not to go through the courtyards as there could be a police ambush waiting for the protesters. On Pushkin Avenue, we walk as slowly and calmly as we can, pretending to be a young family: you are holding a white plastic bag full of groceries, and I press close to you. Military vehicles leisurely drive by.

At home we learn that two Belarusian philosophers, a young family like us, have been detained today near Niamiha street.

October 17–18, the launch of our books
  at a literary festival in Minsk:

We decide to go to your event a few hours early to look around the bookfair. On our way, we read on the internet about the students gathering to march against the state violence. The violence is used against them. The police beat and detain them in the street, just behind the windows where the bookfair guests can see. The masked men wield their batons over the backs and heads of the youngsters, dragging them into blue minibuses without license plates. You ask to go outside, sit down on a bench with your face in your hands, and I silently stroke your back. Suddenly you weep, it lasts for some minutes and then stops. Your face is wet from rain and tears: "I can't take in so much evil."

We take a bus to the mall, where I read the newsfeed about the student march while you go to the WC. The march was dispersed, a lot of people were detained. You feel better after vomiting.

It is nice at the festival. A lot of people attend your discussion. Handsome and confident, you are on the stage speaking about your book, about our dark times, about the role of the writer. People listen, asking questions, and clap. Afterward, around fifty people stand in line with your book in hand, waiting for a moment with their favorite writer.

My new poetry book was published a few days before the election. It was the worst time: no one is interested in a tiny poetry book when the main news is deaths, beatings, and detentions. But there is no other time.

There are just a few people at my event, no questions, a couple of books bought. I get upset. Ania, who is the moderator of the discussion, decides to join the demonstration outside, on Partisans Avenue.

All the guilt, lack of readership, and despair become so unbearable on my shoulders that this time I start weeping by the Philharmonic Hall, where

I read my poems in the summer. Now it's you who are stroking my back in the freezing October cold. On the Telegram app, we watch the violent dispersions of peaceful demonstrations and go home.

October 25:

The authorities block all central squares and main avenues to prevent large gatherings, so each Sunday we get to walk through smaller, often less familiar streets. Each demonstration turns into a city tour. Today we spent the day walking in a large crowd of marchers and ended up at a friend's apartment. I feel guilty in a safe place, with food and wine. In the evening, our beautiful route transformed into a hunting ground for the peaceful marchers. With police cordons everywhere, people seek refuge in the homes of strangers. In the most shocking video posted on Telegram, the riot police break into an apartment where several dozens of people are hiding and, as the owner cries and pleads on her knees, they violently take out all the men they find.

November 1–2:

Today's manifestation has been dedicated to Dziady (Forefathers; the Day of the Dead), which is celebrated on the second of November. It is also dedicated to one of the bloodiest events in the history of Belarus, "The Night of the Executed Poets." During only one October night, from the twenty-ninth to the thirtieth in 1937, 130 Belarusian intellectuals were killed and buried by Soviet authorities in the Kurapaty forest near Minsk. The truth about the mass graves was revealed only at the end of the 1980s, the first manifestation there was dispersed by Soviet authorities. Now there is a memorial for the Stalinist regime's victims: hundreds of wooden crosses remind us of the hundreds of thousands murdered there from 1937 to1941.

Once in August, when it was not so dangerous to show a victory sign to the cars going by, we took part in an action called the Chain of Repentance. The idea was to form a human chain along the road from Kurapaty, the mass grave of the victims of the Stalinist regime, to Akrescina, a place where peaceful protesters were detained, beaten, and tortured by Lukashenka's regime. The unbroken line was thirteen kilometers long.

Today the two of us can neither work nor talk. We sit in different parts of the room, holding our smartphones in our hands, crazily scrolling the news that is too hard to read and to watch, sighing in turn.

Taken. Me.

These are two messages I suddenly get from my brother at 16:13. Then a minute later from his girlfriend: *Pecia is taken.* I get cold imaging him in blood on the floor of the prison van.

But we share a few more messages:

16:26 *Driven somewhere.* (Pecia)
16:27 *Have you been beaten?* (Me)
16:28 *Not yet* (Pecia)

His girlfriend was with him at the field not far from Kurapaty memorial when the police in black and green drove in their minibuses onto the lawn and started hunting for people. I was looking at the surreal photos of the manhunt in the news feed at the very moment when Pecia was captured.

In Belarus, we know the checklist "What to do when your relative has been detained." First, inform the human rights organization or the volunteer initiative about the detention (full name, date of birth, where detained). Second, join the Telegram channel *Lists of the detainees in Akrescina_ Žodzina_Baranaviči,* where the name of your relative or friend could be mentioned. When the rallies are over, Belarusians always look through those long lists of the detained. You are sure to find the names of a dozen people you know. Third, call all the police stations he or she could be in (though in most cases they won't tell you anything). And when you finally know where your relative is, try to pack and pass them a parcel (required medicine, warm clothes, change of underwear, some food, toothpaste and toothbrush, toilet paper—nothing is provided in the jails, not even a mattress with a pillow), but most likely, the parcel will not be accepted.

Only relatives are allowed to give the parcels to the detained. So I go to the white gate and press the button. A young male voice somewhere in the depth of the building informs us that yes, Pecia is here, and no, they do not take parcels.

Around 23:00 the police station officer comes out through the gate, he has a paper in his hand, a list of the detainees. He asks why we are standing here and reassures everybody that "nobody was tortured in the police station." Despite his reassurance three ambulance brigades have been called. Somebody is being transferred to a hospital.

A young woman comes out of the gate, limping, as her friends rush to her and start hugging her. Her face is red from tears, her leg is wounded. We ask her about Pecia, a musician with long hair and a drum. "Ah, he is there in the corner. He is okay, he has not been beaten."

The next day we are at the Žodzina detention center. The court hearings are organized right here and are closed: no lawyers, no timetable, no names of the judges. We hope that Pecia can get a fine, since there are more detainees than the center can house. Police have no choice but to free up space.

We return to Minsk when it's already dark. In the car, we are silent and serious. Pecia has been lucky, we all have been lucky, knock on wood. And hundreds remain in overcrowded jails in awful conditions, beaten, denied medical help. Prisoners with Covid-19 are moved around to different cells to spread the virus. People like us stand in long lines in Minsk, Žodzina, Baranavičy, and Mahiliou with their prison parcels of no more than five kilos.

P.S. Pecia will be arrested again, on August 2, 2021, in a carefully planned police operation with drones and automatic weapons. He will be among a group of musicians celebrating a friend's birthday. The detained musicians will face criminal charges for performing during the summer protests.

March 11, 2021:

Our new home is our castle. The castle is called Cerrini and is situated on a mountain, Schloßberg, in the center of the Austrian city of Graz. We've been invited here by Kulturvermittlung Steiermark for a half-year residency.

We came to Graz in November 2020, about two weeks after Raman Bandarenka was killed. He had been severely beaten by masked people in the yard of his own home and died in the hospital the next day.

The place where Raman was beaten to death is known as the Square of Change. It is an ordinary yard surrounded by newly built apartment blocks with a transformer vault in the center. The residents named their yard the Square of Change after the elections, held gatherings in the front of the transformer vault, and got known nationwide. Raman was murdered because he came outside to ask the masked strangers why they were cutting off the white-and-red ribbons that decorated the fence. Because of the ribbons he was tortured in the car on the way to the police station, then his maimed body was thrown on the porch, and the police officer called an ambulance to take him to the hospital, where he fell into a coma and died.

We were aghast. Anyone could have been in Raman's place. Anyone who would defend the neighborhood where he or she lives. Transformer vaults are found by the thousands in Minsk and other cities and towns; these ugly concrete constructions have become the real symbol of the transformation of power for Belarusian people.

The transformer vault at the Square of Change was the tribune of resistance and the battlefield as well. It all started with two male figures with their arms raised, DJs of Change as everybody called them. These two brave young men put on an old protest song, "We Want Change," at one of the state demonstrations two days prior to the elections, lost their jobs, and were detained by the police at once. Some days later their portraits appeared on the wall of the transformer vault. When the masked men in black painted over them, the two figures were painted again. They were destroyed again, and again restored on the gray wall of the vault. Did these transformations take place twenty times? Thirty times? OMON started guarding the transformation vault day and night to prevent people from painting on it. It sounds absurd, but that's our reality—one that any dystopian author would be envious of.

The day after Raman's death, the whole yard became a sanctuary. Ribbons, candles, flowers, posters, photos of Raman, amateur-drawn portraits of him were placed on the walls and fence. I put flowers under the poster with the names of those murdered since August:

Aliaksandr Tarajkouski
Henadz Šutau
Aliaksandr Vihor
Mikita Kryucou
Aliaksandr Budnicki
Kanstancin Šyšmakou
Raman Bandarenka

Around a thousand people were standing and walking in the yard under a light November rain. Some of them were telling their stories: about escaping the police or, otherwise, about their long days in detention.

The next day the memorial was destroyed by the riot police. Every ribbon, every placard, every flower was ripped out in order to wipe any sign of public mourning. People who were guarding the memorial with their bodies were arrested and put into prison. Dozens managed to hide inside the apartment blocks nearby. The locals were hiding them. They had to lie on the floor without moving, without turning on the lights, without drinking or eating, without using a proper bathroom as the riot police were searching for them, apartment after apartment, until noon the next day.

Two Belarusian female journalists who had been live streaming from the Square of Change that day were found by the police in one of the apartments. They got two years in prison for "coordinating the protests."

On that day you and I were not there. We had our own rally in our neighborhood. The idea was to make the demonstrations decentralized, forcing the police to stretch their resources. Although the tickets to Vienna had already been bought, I insisted we go outside, it was impossible to stay at home. When we came nearer to Pushkin Avenue, we saw military vehicles, barbed wire, and about a hundred riot policemen fully hidden behind metal shields. With these metal shields they planned to block anyone from proceeding, as though somebody would walk unarmed against their army. Sometimes I think that they are fighting with imaginary enemies. They must be wishing for real rivals, worthy of their weapons, worthy of their vehicles and their military toys. But, unfortunately, they've got us: sissy Belarusian people who walk with flowers and posters, like fools.

During our first days in Graz, all I could feel was guilt. Guilt for being free. Guilt for being safe. I followed the news, and the pain was strong, and the fear inside did not want to disappear for a long time. Even now, after four months of life abroad, I have dreams about running and hiding from the police. Sometimes I manage to escape them while dreaming. Sometimes I have to wake up in order to escape.

КАМЕНЬ СТРАХУ

Мне страшна.
Я ўрэшце дома.

Я атрымала ў спадчыну
свой страх —
сямейную рэліквію,
каштоўны камень,
які перадаецца
ад пакалення да пакалення.

Наш круглы радавы валун,
некалі скрадзены
з панскага поля.

Камень не мае рота,
не здольны ні крыкнуць,
ні сказаць.
Ён бяспамятны,
заўжды ў зародку,
усё, што ён умее, —
марудна і няўмольна
расці.

Мы кормім камень па чарзе
праз доўгую пупавіну роду:
прабабулі і прадзядулі,
дзядулі і бабулі,
маці з бацькам,

THE STONE OF FEAR

I'm scared.
I'm home.

I have been handed down a trust fund
of fear—
a family heirloom,
passed
generation to generation,

our round family stone,
stolen
from the landlord's field.

This stone has no mouth,
it can neither scream
nor talk.
This stone has no memory,
an eternally slow-growing
embryo.

One by one, we feed this stone

great-grandmothers and great-grandfathers,
grandfathers and grandmothers,
mothers and fathers,
now that I'm grown—
it's my turn.

The rules of nursing the stone are simple:

а вось і я вырасла —
цяпер мая чарга.

Правілы догляду простыя:
— спачатку ты носіш
камень на сэрцы,
ён п'е тваю кроў і
смокча жыццёвыя сокі.
Камень адвучыць цябе дыхаць
на поўныя грудзі;

— потым дай каменю
ўзняцца вышэй,
зручна захраснуць у горле
і цадзіць твае словы.
Камень адвучыць цябе
гаварыць тое, што хочаш;

— і вось страх выбіраецца вонкі,
абвіваецца каменнаю пупавінай
вакол шыі, вешаецца табе на грудзі,
твая вечная процівага.

— Ах, якая прыгажосць! Гэта ў вас ад бабулі?
— Так.
— Вы ж толькі яго беражыце.
— Абавязкова.

1. Use the stone
to make your heart heavy.
The stone will help you unlearn
how to breathe with a full chest;

2. Let the stone
rise until it's stuck in your throat
sucking on your words.
The stone will help you unlearn
how to say what needs to be said.

3. Watch the fear emerge
wrapped in the umbilical stone
around your neck, hung
with the umbilical stone on your chest,
your eternal counterweight.

—How pretty! Is this your grandma's?
—Yes.
—Take good care of it.
—Always.

НА ГАРОДЗЕ ПРАБАБУЛЯЎ

Бабулечкі, прабабулечкі, пра-прабабулечкі
маленькія, празрыстыя, пухам
зямлі ахінутыя, хукаюць у рукі,
шэпчуць, на вушы мне пасеўшы,
сваё адсеяўшы:
Вось табе агарод,
Вось табе каляндар.
Бяры і сей!

Слухаюся вас, бяру і сею.
Але на маім агародзе ўзыходзяць
толькі трава чырвоная,
толькі туга зялёная,
толькі шэрыя вершы,
што смярдзяць віною ды сорамам.
                    Вам за мяне ці сорамна?

Бабулечкі, прабабулечкі, пра-прабабулечкі
маленькія і празрыстыя,
перад Богам чыстыя
шэпчуць, на вушы мне пасеўшы,
сваё адсеяўшы:
Вось табе агарод,
Вось табе каляндар,
Бяры й рабі!

Слухаюся вас, бяру і раблю,
сыплю зерне ў сухую зямлю.
Але на маім агародзе ўзыходзяць

In the Garden of Great-Grandmothers

Grandnanas, great-grandmamas, great-great-grandparents,
itty-bitty, transparent, dressed
in earth fluff, puffing into their palms,
they perch on my ears and tweet:
Here's your field.
Here's your calendar.
Sow, girl!

I'm so for it. I farm.
But in my field grow only
red grass,
green grief
that reeks of guilt and shame, and gray verses.

Grandnanas, great-grandmamas, great-great-grandparents,
transparent and itty-bitty,
pure before the Lord,
they perch on my ears and tweet:
Here's your field.
Here's your calendar.
Work, girl.

Okay, I throw
seeds into the dry soil.
But in my field grow only
red grass,
green grief,

толькі трава чырвоная,
толькі туга зялёная,
толькі пустазельныя словы,
толькі вершы палыновыя.

ill weeds,
mud words.

What to do with this field, grandmamas?
What to do, grandmamas, with this calendar?

ЦЫРК

Я нарадзілася
з вандроўным цыркам унутры.
З цыркам, толькі падумай,
у палескай вёсцы.
Жанглёры, акрабаты,
барадатыя жанчыны . . .
Які сорам!

Вандроўны цырк
рос разам са мной,
як ваўчаня, што хоча мяса,
яны ўсе шукалі феерверкаў
і шырокіх дарог.
А тут
бураковыя палі,
каларадскія жукі,
народныя прыкметы.

Я хавала свой цырк
між старонак кніг,
як гербарый.
Жанглёраў, акрабатаў,
барадатых жанчын
я выпроствала
ў спадзеве высушыць
іхнія прагныя целы.

Але цыркачы
адмаўляліся гінуць,
яны раслі і мацнелі

CIRCUS

I was born with a traveling circus
inside me.
Unfeasible: a circus
in a swamp village.
Jugglers, acrobats,
a bearded lady.
Wow, embarrassing.

The traveling circus
grew with me,
demanded meat and fireworks,
demanded better roads.
But the swamp begot
fields of beets,
potato beetles,
indigenous proverbs.

I flattened my circus
between book pages,
like an herbarium.
I drained the jugglers, acrobats,
and bearded ladies
of their lust.

But they refused to dry out,
they grew fat under the blankets of pages.
They grew strong.

They learned

пад коўдрай старонак,
на калорыях літар, у шатры майго цела.

Яны вучыліся
цыркавым хітрыкам,
як вучацца качаняты,
кураняты, парсючкі.

І калі набраліся сіл,
знайшлі драбіны,
накрэмзалі мапу —
калі змаглі ўсё тое,
чаго хацелі й што мусілі . . .

Цыркачы мяне скралі.
Цыркачы мяне з'елі.

Цыркачы адкрылі
нарэшце ўва мне
свой вандроўны цырк.

circus tricks
from piglets and chickens.

When they were ready,
they found a ladder,
they drafted a map.

They kidnapped me.
They ate me.

Then they set up
inside me
their traveling circus.

БАБУЛІ

мяне стрыглі каротка
як хлопчыка
ніхто не ведаў
што свае тоўстыя цяжкія косы
ты адпісала мне

мяне вучылі казаць табе «вы»
быццам ты была не адна
ва ўласным целе

бо як сама ты змагла б
вынесці тое
што мне страшна ўявіць

але страшна было табе
ў сцюдзёным балоце
пад цяжарам
мокрых кос

маё імя — атожылак
твайго імя
зялёныя семкі маіх вачэй
вырасталі з тваіх

але я
твой скарб
прадала
                    за ссохлы
драбок свабоды
абрэзала
                    даўгую і тоўстую

Umbilical

my hair was always
cut short
so nobody knew
that you left me
your thick heavy braids

I was taught to address you with a plural "You"
as if there was more than one person
in your body

otherwise, how could you
have endured
your frightening life
alone

frightened, you hid
in the swamp of ice
under the weight
of wet braids

my name is a mirror
of your name
the green seeds of my eyes
grew out of yours

but I
sold
your inheritance
            for a dry

пупавіну валосся

думала скінула
цяжар

але і нябачную
яе напаўняе
памяць

тры гады мы прабавілі поруч
а потым выправіліся
ў розныя падарожжы
ты пад зямлёю
я па зямлі

дзве манеты халодныя
на тваіх павеках бабуля
карункі яловых лапак
на саматканых абрусах
і разарваныя каралі
твайго голасу
звіняць россыпам гукаў
і не збіраюцца ў словы

зямля — гэта нашае мора
адцяўшы пупавіну
касы
ты ў лодцы драўлянай
сплываеш
да самага цэнтру зямлі

далей ад засланага снегам дзірвану
далей ад сухой і шорсткай травы
далей ад пожняў і ад азімых

crumb of freedom
I cut
        long and thick
umbilical hair

I thought I unburdened
myself

but even invisible
the braid grows
with memory

we spent three years together
and then headed out
in two opposite directions
you under the earth
and me onto the earth

two cold coins
on your eyelids
the green lace of pine paws

our fields are our sea
Having cut
the umbilical braid
you are inside a wooden boat
sailing
toward the navel of the earth

far from the snow-choked fields
far from the dry and embittered grass

далей ад комінаў і ад крыжоў

туды дзе цёпла і земляныя птушкі
пяюць танюткімі галасамі
што кожную з нас
аднойчы падхопіць лодка

і панясе

far from hayfields and winter crops
far from chimneys and crosses

ЦЕЛА ПАЭТКІ

Цела паэта належыць яго радзіме.
Абяздоленая зямля прамаўляе ротам паэта,
Вочы паэта бачаць несправядлівасць пакутаў,
А вушы чуюць крыкі нявіннай ахвяры.
Валасы паэта становяцца дуба,
Ногі паэта прарастаюць дубамі,
А далоні паэта сціскаюцца ў кулакі.
І ў яго жылах закіпае кроў:
        як можна дапусціць столькі гора?!

Бясспрэчна, цела паэта належыць яго радзіме.
Хіба ўмее радзіма нешта сказаць без яго?!

Радзіма!
А ці трэба табе маё цела, цела паэткі?
У мяне такая ж гарачая кроў,
Рукі і ногі,
Вочы мае бачаць шмат і вушы чуюць,
І мой рот не меншы за рот паэта!

Маўчыш, адварочваешся?
Бо думаеш, ты такая, як я?
Ты не хочаш быць моцнай, радзіма,
Я ўгадала?
Ты хочаш, каб паэт сказаў за цябе,
Каб шкадаваў цябе,
Каб выціраў табе слёзы,
І ўсім пяяў,
        як ты пакутуеш

BODY OF A POETESS

A poet's body belongs to his motherland.
Motherland speaks through the poet's mouth.
Poet's eyes see how unfairly it suffers.
Poet's ears hear the agony of the innocent.
Poet's hair stands on end,
poet's legs burst into oaks,
poet's hands fold into fists.

Motherland! Can you speak for yourself
without poet's help?

And would you like my body, the body of a poetess?
My blood is as hot,
I got hands, legs,
seeing eyes, hearing ears,
my mouth is no smaller than any poet's,
Motherland!

You don't wish to respond, motherland. You turn away.
Perhaps we are too much alike.
You'd rather be weak, wouldn't you,
motherland?
You want poet to speak for you,
to pity you,
to wipe your tears,
to sing odes
to your suffering
and world-famous resilience?

і якая ты малайчына? . .
Праўда, радзіма?

Але ты мяне не слухаеш,
Ты зноў скардзішся свайму паэту.

Цела паэткі табе не патрэбна.
І я забіраю яго сабе.

Even now you are not listening.
Tsk-tsk: you are whining to your poet.

No, you don't need the body of a poetess.
It's mine.

MOTHER TONGUE

У мяне мамін чырвоны язык.
Гутаперчавы хлопчык.
Ён

    гнецца ва ўсе бакі.
Ён

    скача праз кола зубоў.
Ён

    узлятае

з мокрай арэны сківіцы

    да паднябеннага купала.
(Зноў гэты цырк!..)

Мама, у мяне ў роце
твой чырвоны язык.
Ты бачыла,
як я вучылася
на ім гаварыць,
як аблізвала
твае салодкія словы,
як прагна смактала
твой грудны голас,

як вымагала: яшчэ.

Мама, у мяне ў роце
твой чырвоны язык.
Я піла тваё малако,
каб ён рос,

MOTHER TONGUE

I have my mother's red tongue.
A nimble boy,
he flexes
       this way and that.
He
       jumps through the hoops of teeth.
He flies up

from the wet arena of the jaw
to the palatal dome
(there's this circus again).

Mama, in my mouth
is your red tongue.
You watched me
learn
to use him,
lick
your sweet words,
suck
your bosom voice,

and ask for more.

Mama, in my mouth
is your red tongue.
I drank your milk
so he would grow,
gain weight,

каб набіраў кілаграмы,
каб вучыўся трымаць галоўку
ў сваёй слінявай калысцы,
каб пачаў поўзаць
ад шчакі да шчакі.

Каб урэшце пачуўся
яго дзіцячы лепет.

Мама, у мяне ў роце
твой чырвоны язык.
Ён так і не вырас,
ён так і не стаў сапраўдным
мужчынам. Хлопчык,
які ў людзі адзяваецца
дзяўчынкай.

Мама, я вучуся гаварыць
штодня. Я вучуся гаварыць
чужымі для цябе
мовамі, пра чужыя для цябе
рэчы. Ты падарыла мне жыццё –
а я адкрыла ў ім школу
замежных моў.

Але язык у маім роце
ўсё роўна адзін.
І ён твой.

learn to hold his head
in the salivating cradle
so he could crawl
from cheek to cheek,

so we could hear his
baby patter.

Mama, in my mouth
is your red tongue.
He has failed to grow,
has failed to man up.

Mama, I learn to speak
every day. In a language foreign
to you, I learn to speak
about things
foreign to you. You gave me life
and I opened inside it a school
of foreign languages.

ЧОРТ

Сад жывы, як і ўсё наўкола. Я чую, як ён удыхае і выдыхае. Я бачу, як ад яго дыхання асыпаюцца долу круглыя пялёсткі. Мы крочым па вузкай вытаптанай сцежцы, а паабапал -- крываватыя яблыні. Раскінуўшы драўляныя рукі, яны застылі ў няручных позах, быццам заспетыя за дзіцячай гульнёй: "Замры!". Калі б стаяла зіма, я, магчыма, спужалася б іх тонкіх і кручкаватых, быццам на агромністы аркуш снегу наклееных, чорных канцавінаў, але вясною, яблыні зусім не страшныя. Прывітанне, яблыні!

Дзед адводзіць нас на прыпынак, цягнучы цяжкую торбу з яшчэ зімовымі запасамі. Тата трымае сястру на руках, а я ля мамы іду сама. Выходныя амаль скончыліся, заўтра бацькам на працу, а нам у дзіцячы садок. Дзед гучна цалуе і абдымае ўнучак, дачку і зяця ды вяртаецца назад па той самай сцежцы да сваёй самотнай хаты. Мы махаем яму ўслед, пакуль яго тонкі абрыс не распускаецца між галін у яблыневай квецені.

На прыпынку мы чакаем аўтобус, які ўсё не едзе. Прыпынак – гэта зялёная драўляная лаўка без спінкі, мы з сястрой сядзім на ёй і гайдаем нагамі.

— Перастаньце! – сварыцца мама. – Чорта на назе калышаце!

Але на сандаліках мы нікога не бачым, і хіба чорта можа быць адразу два, ці нават чатыры?

— Чэрці нябачныя, – тлумачыць мама, а тата паглядвае то на гадзіннік, то на металічную шыльду з раскладам, то на пустую дарогу.

— Ігнаценкі сёння гарод садзілі, — кажа мама, апускаючыся побач на лаву. — Люда, Іванавага сына жонка, з Прыпяці званіла, казала, што Васіля сёння сярод ночы вызвалі. У іх там аварыя ці пажар на атамнай станцыі. Вызвалі тушыць.

ROCKING THE DEVIL

The garden is alive, as is everything else around here. I hear it breathe. I see round petals float down with each exhale. We trot on a narrow path amid writhed apple trees. If right now were winter, I might have gotten frightened of their thin wooden hooks, but we are in spring. Greetings, apple trees!

Grandpa walks us to a bus stop, lugging a heavy bag with supplies left from the winter. Dad carries my sister in his arms, and I keep up next to mama. The weekend is almost gone, tomorrow our parents are off to work, and we are back at the state daycare. Grandpa's kisses are loud. He hugs us all and walks along the same path, back to his sad hut. We wave to him until his thin figure dissolves amid the blossoms.

We wait for a bus that is as always late. The bus stop is a green wooden bench, backless, where my sister and I sit swinging our feet.

"Stop it!" mama nags. "Stop rocking the devil with your feet!" We look at our sandals and see no devil there.

"Devils are invisible," mama explains, while dad keeps turning between his wristwatch and the empty road.

"Today, the Ihnatsenkys have planted their vegetables," mama says and sits down next to us on the bench. "Lyuda, the wife of Ivan's son, telephoned from Prypiat, said that Vasil was called in the middle of the night. There's some accident at the power plant. He was called to put out a fire."

"Probably nothing serious, no?"

"Probably. He was called urgently, so they had to plant the garden without him." Suddenly, the sky darkens. The wind pulls at the grass around the bus stop, the road dust, the apple trees in the gardens. The gardens try to resist the wind, but they choke on their own rage. The petals fly with the wind, dust rises and throws itself at us, the grass whisks itself into menacing switches. Frightened with all that devil's work, my sister and I finally stop swinging our feet.

— Ну, можа, нічыво сур'ёзнага.

— Можа. Но што-та срочнае. Самі гарод пасадзілі, без іх.

Неба, што яшчэ колькі хвілінаў таму было светлым, раптам цямнее. Хмары распырскваюць змрок. Вецер злуецца і сварыцца на траву ля прыпынку, на дарожны пыл, на яблыні ў садзе. Сад пачынае і сам задыхацца ад злосці і размахваць галінамі. Пялёсткі не хочуць яго слухацца, рвуцца за ветрам, пыл падымаецца з зямлі і кідаецца на нас, трава ля лаўкі грозна матае мяцёлкамі. Тады мы з сястрой, напужаныя гэтай чартаўнёй, пераглядваемся і ўрэшце перастаем гайдаць нагамі.

На пяску прасёлка з'яўляецца першая цёмная пляма, затым, крыху наводдаль, другая. І вось іх ужо дзясяткі, сыплюцца на нашыя голыя галовы. Цёплая вада праціне кофту, сукенку, залазіць пад калготкі і ў сандалі. Нам усё роўна не ўратавацца – побач ні даху, ні дрэва, ні нават чырвонага дзіцячага парасона з маіх мар. Таму замест таго, каб гайдаць нагамі чарцей, мы з сястрой падхопліваемся з лаўкі і радасна пачынаем бегаць наўкол, падстаўляючы кароткія языкі пад вясновыя кроплі. Мама зноў просіць нас супакоіцца, і мы зноў не слухаемся.

Нікому пакуль невядома, колькі бруду, бяды і смерці ў гэтых нявінных кроплях, у гэтым познакрасавіцкім дажджу, што проста цяпер будуе з неба ў зямлю шэры непранікальны мур, назаўжды аддзяляючы наша мінулае ад цяперашняга.

І раптам, гэтак жа нечакана, дождж спыняецца на паўслове, хмары паўзком уцякаюць на поўдзень, толькі сінія пяткі маланкамі бліскаюць над лесам. Яблыні ціха трасуць расквечанымі галінамі, спрабуюць скінуць шкодныя кроплі, але яны ўжо прасачыліся ў кару, у пялёсткі, праніклі ў яшчэ ледзь назначаныя завязі.

А вось і аўтобус, мокры, як мы. Да Пірак 25 кіламетраў. Праз кроплі на шыбах я заўважаю, як галіны махаюць нам услед: "Бывайце!" Ці вернемся?

First a dark spot appears on the dust road. Then, slightly farther, another. Now it's pouring over our heads. The warm water soaks our cardigans, dresses, tights, and sandals. We have nowhere to hide. So, my sister and I start running in the storm, sticking out our short tongues for the drops of spring rain. Mama asks us to calm down, but we don't listen.

In that moment, nobody yet knows how much suffering and death are carried in those innocent raindrops, which seem to be building a wall that will forever separate us from our past lives.

The rain stops midsentence, as suddenly as it began. The clouds crawl north, and blue heels of lightning strike above the forests. Apple trees tremble, trying to shake off disastrous raindrops, but they have already seeped under the bark, into the petals, into the new buds.

Here comes the bus, wet like us. twenty-five kilometers to Pirkie. Between the trails of raindrops on the bus windows, I watch the branches waving to us: "Farewell!"

1986

Мы не змаглі забраць вас з сабою,
       бязногія нашы дамы.
Не змаглі ўзваліць вас на плечы
і вынесці на сабе,
       свежаўзараныя гароды.
Могілкі, мы не здолелі выкапаць
з карэннем
       вашы крыжы
і перасадзіць іх
       у чыстую глебу.

Яблыневыя сады,
стуліўшы бела-ружовыя павекі,
вы замоўклі, з надзеяй
       чакаючы на наша вяртанне.
І калі, цэзіем аплодненыя,

чырванню наліліся вашы завязі,
толькі здзічэлыя й згаладалыя кошкі
       па зорках
       вярнуліся назад,
але яблыкаў вашых
       яны ўсё роўна не елі.

Яблыкі ападалі й гнілі, крыжы
высыхалі
       без нашых слёз,
гароды заблытваліся ў пустазеллі
і заміралі.

А нашы дамы старэлі,
дамы гублялі

1986

We couldn't take you with us,
　　　　our legless houses.
We couldn't carry you out on our shoulders,
　　　　our freshly plowed fields.
Our graves,
we couldn't dig out
　　　　the deep roots of your crosses
in order to transplant them
　　　　into new soil.

Apple gardens,
closed pink-white eyelids,
　　　　silent, hoping for our return.
When, impregnated with cesium,

your buds grew red,
starved feral cats
　　　　followed the stars back home,
but didn't touch
　　　　your fruit.

Apples fell and rotted,
　　　　thirsty for our tears,
crosses dried up, gardens
　　　　got lost in the weeds
and grew silent.

Our houses aged,
　　　　losing their minds and memories.

ад гора

розум і памяць.

Чужыя людзі вырвалі

з цвікамі

дошкі падлогі,

знялі са сцен пыльныя дываны з паўлінамі,

скралі ўсе нашы   хворыя рэчы,

хворыя рэчы,

якія ніхто не мог вылечыць,

рэчы, якія самі маўчалі

пра сваю хваробу.

Рэчы, без якіх нашы дамы

зморшчыліся і счаўрэлі.

Праз многа гадоў

мы прыехалі ў госці,

і толькі

могілкавыя крыжы

памахалі нам вышываным ашмоццем

старых рушнікоў.

Ні дамы,

ні гароды,

ні яблыні

нас не прызналі.

І як ні ўпрошвалі

нашы добрыя продкі

са сваіх свежапрыбраных магіл,

ні дамы,

ні гароды,

ні яблыні

нам нічога не даравалі.

Strangers tore out the floor,
took down from the walls our dusty carpets,
stole all of our sick belognings,
        sick, uncurable belongings,
things silent about their sickness.

When after many years
we came back for a visit,
only cemetery crosses
        waved at us with the rags
of their embroided towels.

Neither houses,
        nor gardens,
                nor apple trees
recognized us.

No matter how hard
our forgiving dead
begged them from their freshly
cleaned graves,
neither houses, nor gardens,
nor apple trees
forgave us.

ПОЛЕ I

Ваша поле шырокае і лянівае
Раскінулася, як шэрая бабская хустка.
Яна вас грэе,
Яна вас трымае ля сябе,
Маленькіх і працавітых,
Прывязаўшы за ногі ў брудных
гумовых ботах, за пазбіваныя пальцы,
за цёмныя ад сонца шыі.
Поле скруціла вас, змусіла да незлічоных
паклонаў. Вашы рукі – вось
вашы сапраўдныя думкі,
заблытаваюцца ў сырых разорах,
разгладжваюць і лашчаць
маршчыны ўладнай гаспадыні.

Я ваша дзіця,
поле мае і на мяне права.
Але мае ногі падкошваюцца,
Рукі не хочуць гладзіць разоры.
Я падаю і рыю тунэль,
Я ўцякаю з роднай зямлі
пад зямлю, пад грузнае
цела поля.
Куды я выпаўзу
з-пад гэтых цёмных неахопных грудзей,
з-пад гэтага цяжкага чэрава,
з пад гэтых урадлівых угноеных сцёгнаў:
да мора, да зораў, да гор?
Хто сустрэне мяне па той бок тунэлю:
Бог, вада ці драпежная дзюба?!

MOTHERFIELD (1)

Motherfield, you are wide and lazy
like an old woman's scarf.
You keep us bundled.
You keep us at hand,
short and hardworking,
you grip us by our muddy
rubber boots, by our deformed fingers,
by the necks darkened in the sun.
Motherfield has twisted us, forced us into
prostration. Our hands
are our only thoughts.

I'm a child of my motherland.
Motherfield owns me.
But my legs are limp,
my hands refuse to smooth out furrows.
I dig a tunnel, I run
from my native soil
into the underbelly
of the field.
Where does this heavy womb
lead? Where do these fertilized thighs
open? At the sea, the stars, the hills?
Is it safe to poke out?

Няўмольнае поле
пакарала мяне за ўцёкі —
зрабіла
сляпою краціхай.

Motherfield
has punished me for the escape—
it has transformed me
into a blind mole.

ПОЛЕ II

Штогод поле робіцца маладой.
Пад тонкім вэлюмам снегу,
пад строгім наглядам традыцый.
Яго расчэсваюць граблямі,
разгладжваюць плугамі
і апладняюць.

Поле расце. Поле цвіце.
Закусвае сухія вусны разораў,
слухае сэрцы маленькіх бульбін
пад кожным калівам.

Поле не можа ўстаць,
ляжыць распластаная, капрызная
ў пустазеллі й бацвінні.
Просіць сонца. Просіць вады.

Увосень парадзіха ўздрыгне
ад першага холаду,
скаланецца апошняй грымотай;
і паскачуць, пасыплюцца
ў кашы яе круглыя дзеці.

Апусцелае поле выдыхне.
і заплюшчыць земляныя вочы.

Спі спакойна, старая.
Хутка зноў прачынацца.

MOTHERFIELD (2)

Every year the motherfield is a bride.
Under a thin muslin of snow,
under the strict supervision of tradition.
It is smoothed with rakes,
combed with plows,
inseminated.

The pasture grows thick. The pasture glows,
listening to the many-hearted beating
of potato plants.

Pasture cannot rise.
It lies spread out, finicky about weeds.
Asks for sunlight. Asks for water.

In the fall, laboring pasture quivers
from the first frost,
shudders in the last spasm,
and out spill into baskets
its round newborns.

An emptied pasture exhales
and closes its pebbly eyes.

Rest, old motherfield.
A new labor is ahead.

* * *

. . . дзяўчынка, стоячы,
гушкалася на арэлях
і прыгаворвала:
"Каця добрая,
Каця кепская . . .
Каця добрая,
Каця кепская . . ."

Арэлі — уверх,
ледзь не да аблокаў —
добрая.

Арэлі — уніз,
амаль траву кранаюць —
кепская.

Добрая,
кепская.
Добрая,
кепская.

Надакучыла Каці,
і недзе між верхам і нізам,
між аблокамі і травою,
яна выпусціла жалезныя пруты з рук,
зрабіла з арэляў крок наперад
і пабегла босымі пяткамі
па цёплым летнім паветры . . .

Не было ні добрай Каці,
ні кепскай,
ні сумнай,
ні вясёлай . . .
Каця збегла.
Каця змагла.

[A SWINGING GIRL]

A swinging girl
recited:

Katie's good,
Katie's bad,
Katie's good,
Katie's bad.

The swing's up
good.

The swing's down
bad.

Katie's gotten bored
and someplace
between up and down
she let the metal rods go
and stepped forward
across the warm summer air.

There was neither good
nor bad Katie,
neither sad
nor glad Katie.

She ran away.

ПЕРШАМУ ГОРАДУ

Я баюся тваіх дзяцей,
горад Жлобін,
вылітых з металу,
выкармленых
смярдзючымі цыцкамі
                заводу.

Іх цвёрдыя целы
ты загарнуў,
        горад Жлобін,
у штучнае футра
       з галавы да ног.
Кітайскім клеем
         наляпіў ім на футра
белыя вочы.

Але пад пластмасай вачэй
іх металічныя вейкі
              самкнутыя,
іх шырокія сківіцы шчыльна сашчэпленыя,
быццам   дызельныя   вагоны,
быццам   грузавыя   вагоны,
быццам   пасажырскія   вагоны,
што, дрыжучы, імкнуць
            без стомы і сну,
праз чыгуначны вузел
твайго пупа.

Разам расці тваім дзецям,
горад Жлобін,
бегаючы па рэйках,
скачучы праз шпалы,
прагнучы марна цяпла

ZHLOBIN, MY FIRST CITY

I fear your children, Zhlobin,
the steel-cast children
of Zhlobin
nursed by the factory's
smoggy tits.

Zhlobin wrapped
their firm bodies
      into imitation fur.
With the made-in-China glue
      Zhlobin glued onto the fur
white eyes.

Under the plastic eyes
their metal eyelashes
            are locked,
their wide mouths sealed
like   oil   tanks
human   freight   trains
that shiver without sleep
      through the railway junction
of my navel.

The children of Zhlobin grow
jumping over railroad ties,
longing for warmth
in their artificial
rabbit fur,   bear fur,
cat fur,   elephant fur,

ў штучным
заечым,   мядзведжым,
каціным,   слановым,
ружовым і сінім   футры.

Сонца не ведае, дзе ты,
                    горад Жлобін.
У металічнай смузе
ты адводзіш сваіх дзяцей у садок.
У металічным змроку
ты забіраеш сваіх дзяцей назад
у мікрараёны, якія,

калі клічаш іх сярод вуліцы,
адзываюцца толькі на лічбы і мат.

Твае дзеці ўмеюць лічыць, але не ўмеюць чытаць.
Твае дзеці ўмеюць піць, але не ўмеюць есці.
Твае дзеці ўмеюць біць,
Твае дзеці не ўмеюць быць.

Горад Жлобін, ці памятаеш ты мяне?
Штучнае футра маёй плацэнты
дагэтуль
        вісіць на мосце
                    чыгуначнага вакзала.
Мае заечыя вочы
дагэтуль
        раскіданыя пад нагамі
                    на цэнтральным базары
і, як у казцы,
сочаць
за тваім цяперашнім жыццём:

бліскучы метал тваіх дзяцей
не паблякнуў;
поўныя цыцкі заводу,

pink and blue   fur.

The sun doesn't know
where Zhlobin is found.
In the metal smog
Zhlobin takes its children to a daycare.
In the metal twilight
it take its children back
into the public housing

calling them home by their number
and curse.

Your children know how to count, but know not how to read.
Your children know how to drink, but know not how to eat.
Your children know a good whack.

Do you remember me, city of Zhlobin?
The artificial fur of my placenta
still hangs
          on the bridge
                    of the railway station.
My rabbit eyes
are still scattered
                    under feet
                              on the central market,
they watch your ongoing life:

the shiny metal of your children
didn't fade,
the full tits of the factory
still feed the citizens,

каб усіх выкарміць,
усё гэтак жа
       сцэджваюць
              у аблокі
чорнае малако.

А з мяне сочыцца
чырвань іржы.
Мая кроў.

still squeeze into the clouds
their black milk.

Out of me
comes rust.

ВКДШ

цёмна
чырвонае
брыдка
цёплае
мяккае й мокрае
што яшчэ не зрабілася нічым
ні рыбінай
ні бутонам
ні ліпавай ліпкай пупышкай

некім мусіла быць
нічым не стала
нішто стала
не стала

а мусіла быць
што
кім мусіла быць
рыбкай
кветкай
вавёркай
не стала
нішто
стала
боль- ш-ш-ш-ш-ш
чым

-дыш
дышы
народзіш
новае
маладая яшчэ

што?

MSCRRDG

tossed
gross
red
ain't a bud-
dy, stick-
y ain't a thing
ain't a tad-
pole

was supposed to
no support
in part imp not a thin
g

was supposed
to be what
tadpo-
poppy
something m-
uuuuuuuugh
than

hmm . . . embryoo
bry
breathe
still young
you will have
more

what?

МОВА — ТУРМА

Мова — т
урма,
у якую нас пасадзілі
за нежаданне
й няздольнасць
увабраць у сябе ЎСЁ.

Мы прагнем межаў і сценаў,
і калючага дроту радкоў,
каб, кідаючыся на іх
у спробе вырвацца,
адчуць сябе жывымі.

Мы трапляем у мову малымі
і не памятаем іншага жыцця,
акрамя турэмнага,
іншага неба,
акрамя закратаванага,
іншай ежы, акрамя поснай поліўкі
пустых штодзённых размоваў.

Ніхто не пытаўся ў нас,
ці хочам мы нараджацца.
Ніхто не пытаўся ў нас,
ці хочам мы гаварыць.

Памяць трымае нас тут,
і адзіны шлях адсюль —
забыццё.
Але за межамі мовы —
каінава самота,

LANGUAGE IS A PRISON SENTENCE

For our resistance,
for our inability
to absorb the whole world.

We want poems made
out of barbed wire,
so that when we throw ourselves upon them in flight
we might feel alive.

We get sentenced to language as children
and remember no other life,
except for prison life,
no sky,
but the sky behind words,
no food, but the tasteless broth
of thin daily speech.

Nobody asked us
whether we wanted to be born.
Nobody asked us
whether we wanted to learn to speak.

Memory keeps us here,
and the only way out
is oblivion.
But beyond language
is Cain's sadness,
oblivion is a murder.
To escape

бо забыццё — гэта забойства.
Адзін з найстрашнейшых,
з самых непамысных грахоў —
уцячы па сваёй волі
з палону Мовы.

Вызваліцца —
замоўкнуць —
адчуць,
як уздымаюцца
магутныя грудзі Сусвету.

І ў яго разняволеным шуме
не знайсці ніякага сэнсу

from the prison of language
is a great sin.

To escape—
to stop talking—
to feel
the rise and fall
of the great bosom of the world.

Its liberated hum
makes no sense.

АДМОЎНАСЦЬ

Тая мова, на якой я магу гаварыць,
Гэта не мая мова. А тая, на якой хачу гаварыць,
Не ўкладаецца ў словы,
Якія я ведаю,
Не змяшчае вобразы,
Якія я бачу.

Для маёй мовы няма слоўнікаў,
Для яе не сфармулявана правілаў.

Гэта мова для чытання самой сабе,
Мова для чытання з памылкамі,
Бо праверыць няма каму.

Пісаць на ёй я не змагу ніколі.
Калі ты чытаеш гэты верш,
Ты не мой чытач.

NEGATIVE LINGUISTIC CAPABILITY

The language I can speak
is not my language.
The language I wish to speak
isn't contained in words
I know,
isn't contained in images
I see.

For my language there are no dictionaries,
no agreed upon rules.

It's a language for reading my own self,
language for reading with mistakes,
because there is no one to correct me.

I will never write in this language.
If you are reading this poem,
you are not my reader.

ВЫЦІНАНКА

мы з табою пара нажніцаў
рэжам
адзін на дваіх белы аркуш

вырастаюць з яго
белыя дрэвы
белыя кветкі
выкараскваюцца
пачвары
і чэрці
выпростваюць свае
крывыя белыя ногі
і топчуць белыя сцябліны
але папяровыя чэрці
папяровым кветкам
не могуць нашкодзіць

з белага аркуша
вырастае пяшчота
любоў
вырастае сум
і самота
сваркі і звадкі і звон
увушшу
ад маўчання

мы ўмеем усё
парай нажніцаў
мы рэжам
адзін на дваіх белы аркуш

мовы

нараджаем сусвет
вострымі лёзамі
сваіх языкоў

PAPERCUTTING

You and I are a pair of scissors
that cut
the same white piece of paper

Out of this paper, white
trees sprout
white flowers
beasts crawl out
demons stretch their white legs
and topple white stems
but paper beasts
cannot harm
paper flowers

Out of this paper
tenderness sprouts
love
longing sprouts
loneliness
discord and squabbles and ringing
in my ear
from silence

We can do anything
as long as the two of us
scissor
one language

* * *

Мае вершы нюхаюць твае вершы,
быццам сабакі
пад хвастом адзін у аднога,
сустрэўшыся выпадкова
на часопісным развароце.

[MY POEMS SNIFF]

My poems sniff your poems
like two dogs that have met
at the intersection of a magazine spread.

НОВАЯ ВОПРАТКА КАРАЛЯ

Сяджу ў майстэрні фатографа
і слухаю Баха.
На цагляных сценах XIX стагоддзя —
чорна-белыя партрэты
голых мадэляў:
іх вусны, плечы,
грудзі і сцёгны.

А барочная музыка аркестра
ў чорным прайгравальніку
палачкай дырыжора,
быццам іголкай,
праколвае секунду за секундай
і вышывае ў паветры
каляровыя кветкі.
Шыўкі скрыпак, клавіраў і флейтаў
роўна кладуцца
на сцены,
на фота мадэляў,
аздабляючы
матэрыяй часу
пустэчу.

І я думаю,
ці напраўду быў голым кароль,
калі пад літаўры і горны
прыдворнага аркестра
горда ішоў па плошчы,
адчуваючы на сабе
ядваб і аксаміт музыкі,
вытанчанай,
зашпіленай на ўсе гузікі.
А грубы натоўп
яе проста не здолеў
разгледзець.

EMPEROR'S NEW CLOTHES

On the brick wall
of an artist studio,
I look at photographs,
all nudes, black-and-white,
and listen to Bach.

A baton
directing baroque orchestra music
embroiders, like a busy needle,
in the air:
a violin stitch, a flute stitch,
a clavier stitch—covering the air,
dressing the nudes
in the fabric of time.

And I wonder
whether the Emperor was truly naked.

He marched vainly
to the sound of the royal
orchestra, listening
to the music with his whole
body. Dressed in music.

And the crowd laughed like horses
and didn't know better.

НА СЯМЕЙНЫМ ПАДВОРКУ

На цвіках,
намертва ўбітых
у драўляныя сцены
павеці памяці — выцвілыя
анучы крыўдаў,

ні колеру, ні формы,
напаўзбуцвелыя акраўкі
з ваўняным шмаццём карункаў
з апошнім белым гузікам . . .
Гэта каўнер або рукаў?
Хто надзяваў іх на сябе?
І хто пашыў
на стракатлівай машынцы нэндзы?

Да іх прыемна
працягнуць руку
                    ў летняй
                              прахалодзе павеці
кранаючы
                    напаўзабытае,
напаўжывое, кранаючы
напаўбалючае,
як корку бурую
на незагоенай
каленцы.

У змрок павеці неяк
          хтосьці зойдзе
          і з намертва ўбітых
          цвікоў сарве
старыя анучы крыўдаў.

FAMILY THRESHOLD

On the deadly nails
affixed
to the mudroom
of memory—faded
rags of grudges
old garments
recycled for household use

colorless, shapeless,
half-dust
wool lace
last white button.
Was this a collar or a sleeve?
Who wore it?
Who sewed it
on the whirring machine?

In the cool summer mudroom
I like to touch with my fingers
something half-forgotten,
half-living, half-
hurting,
like a scab
on a healing knee.

Someone snatches
the old rags of grudges
nailed deadly
in the dark mudroom.

Саб'е з іх пыл і прах,
угледзіцца
у іх бясформеннасць,
а ўрэшце спаліць
на вогнішчы сваёй гісторыі.

У маёй хай трохі павісяць.

Someone brushes off their dust and ash,
peers into their
shapelessness
and finally burns them in the fire
of their history.

Let mine hang there longer.

ПАСЛЯДОЎНАСЦЬ

1

а пасля
яны елі клубніцы з малаком
пасыпалі іх цукрам і лыжкай лавілі
пунсовыя цвёрдыя цельцы
ягад у жоўтых радзімках зярнятаў

а перад гэтым . . .

а пасля на алавяных лыжках
клубніцы
ляжалі як дзеці
ў белых пялюшках
малака
сцішаныя і малыя

а перад гэтым . . .

а пасля
яны раскрывалі вусны
яны расшчаплялі зубы
яны клалі клубніцы з жоўтымі зоркамі
зярнятаў у яміны ратоў

а перад гэтым . . .

а пасля
яны рухалі сківіцамі

ORDER

1

After that
they ate strawberries with cream,
sprinkling them with sugar, spooning
firm, cardinal-chested berries
covered in yellow dots
of seeds,

and before that . . .

and after that, strawberries
cradled on tin spoons
like babies
in white swaddles
of cream,
calm and small,

and before that . . .

and after that
they reddened their lips,
they unchained their teeth,
they placed strawberries with yellow stars
of seeds into the dugout holes
of their mouths,

and before that . . .

and after that

слодыч сачылася пад язык

чырвань цукровага соку

сцякала ў глотку

рука замірала на імгненне

і, ажыўшы, зноў цягнулася

да збялелых ягад

сканчаўся доўгі ліпеньскі дзень

а перад гэтым . . . а пасля

а перад гэтым . . . а пасля

2

Калі я прыбыў на месца,

ужо была выкапаная вялізная яма,

гэта мог быць стары супрацьтанкавы

роў.

Да ямы іх вялі групамі па 15 чалавек

і выстаўлялі ў шэраг тварамі да стралкоў.

Было загадана, каб адзін стралок

цэліў у грудзі, а другі адпаведна

ў галаву.

Калі сёння ў мяне пытаюцца

пра іншыя дэталі, мушу сказаць,

што, акрамя гэтай паслядоўнасці,

пра той дзень я больш нічога не памятаю.

Па вяртанні з задання я бачыў, як

салдатам 2-га ўзводу на вячэру далі

they wheeled their jaws,
the sweetness seeped under their tongues,
red sugar
dripped into their throats,
a hand paused
and again went
for the berries pale with cream,
a long July daybreak

and before that . . . and after
and before that . . . and after

2
When I arrived there
they'd already dug out a large hole
though it could have been an anti-tank
pit.

Groups of fifteen people were led to the edge
and placed facing the shooters.

One shooter
aimed t the chest, and the second one
at the head. That was the order.

Now, when asked
about other details, I respond that,
besides this order,
I remember nothing of that day.

Upon our return, I saw

клубніцы з малаком.

а пасля

that the soldiers of the second platoon were having dinner—
strawberries with cream.

And after that

ЧЫТАЮ ВЕРШ НА ЧУЖОЙ МОВЕ

ускарaskваюся
на яго вяршыню
стаю аглядаючы прастор
як ваяка-выведніца
з лёгкім заплечнікам
слоўнікавага запасу
за спінай

спрабую
зразумець куды
вядзе гэтая пакручастая
метафара дзе
сканчаецца мяжа
думкі і каму з мёртвых
пакінулі зарослы помнік
на скрыжаванні
гэтых даўгіх радкоў

у ранніх прыцемках неразумення
брыду амаль навобмацак
прыслухоўваюся
да свісцячага і шыпячага
ландшафту страчваю
раўнавагу падаю ў твань
хапаюся за пераклад-
зіну крыху смыляць
далоні ад вострых стрэмак
і мокрая па пояс
іду далей

I READ A POEM IN A FOREIGN LANGUAGE

I climb
its peak
survey the landscape
like a partisan woman
with a light backpack
of word supplies
behind my back

I try
to understand where
this winding metaphor
leads to, where
the border of a thought
ends, and whose gravestone
is left to overgrow
the crossroads
of these long lines

In the twilight of confusion
I wander by tongue
I listen
to the hissing and hushing
landscape, I lose
balance, fall into the bog,
grab onto the bridge
of translation my palms burn
from splinters,
wet up to my waist
I proceed

выведніца-ваяка — дзіўны вобраз
я не люблю вайну але
на тэрыторыі замежнай мовы
я — самотная шпіёнка
і мушу выкрасці сакрэт
гэтых чужых зацягнутых
вільготнаю смугою гор
каб сеўшы на прывал
пасля занатаваць
туманным шыфрам
паэзіі ўласнай

I don't like war but
I approach the territory of a foreign language
as a melancholy spy
I must steal a secret
of these strange hills
under cover of mist
So that later, I can sit down at a rest stop
and write
the script-mist
of my own poetry

ЗІМОЙ

Шлях на працу—адкрыты космас.
Галава—ў скафандры з думак.
Я—першая жанчына-касманаўт
на вуліцы Варанянскага.

WINTER

With my head in the space suit of thoughts,
a walk to the editor's office is open outer space.

I'm the first female astronaut
        on Varanyansky Street.

АЎТАПАРТРЭТ У ВЫГЛЯДЗЕ КОСТАЧКІ АВАКАДА

чым большая костачка
тым хутчэй

       яна прарасце —

я чытала парады
перш чым уткнуць
тры зубачысткі
у цвярдыню яе сцягна

перш чым заглыбіць
шчыльны каўчэг

            зярняці
у шклянку з вадой

з раніцы раптам
лупіна

       лопнула
разламалася

       мясістая костачка

быццам сталі
насупраць адзін аднаго
два сусветы

іх можна было б назваць
тут і там
захад і ўсход
чужое і роднае
урэшце

       яны і мы

SELF-PORTRAIT AS AN AVOCADO SEED

The larger the avocado seed
the sooner it'll sprout

I researched the growing tips
before I stabbed
three toothpicks
into its firm thigh

before I lowered
an ark sealed
hermetically
into a glass of water

by the morning
the shell
       is cracked
the fleshy seed
       split in two

as if two worlds
have come
to a face-off

I could call them
here and there
west and east
mine and not mine
and finally
       us and them

можна было б

калі б не корань
што пачынае расці
між
дзвюх палавінак

калі б не сцябліны
маленькая галава
прыўзнятая над вадою

глядзі
як выпаўзае
хтосьці з каўчэгу
у пошуках новай зямлі

гэта я

one could have

if not for the root
that shoots and grows
between
the two halves

if not for the small head
of a sprout
raised over the water

look:
somebody crawls
out of the ark
in search of a new land

it's me

ЗАБРАЛІ

у чорную шчыліну
бетоннага плота
спрабую разгледзець
насаты профіль
мучыцеля

гэта Дзяржынскі
          вас там дзяржыць
у Бараўлянскім аддзеле міліцыі?
бязрукі Дзяржынскі
завостраным носам
падпісвае вам пратаколы
і адпраўляе з рукамі за спінай
у кайданках ці сцяжках
(з-за плоту не бачна)

у аўтазак
белы і правільны
як халадзільнік?

ЗАБРАЛІ

і вось мы стаім
мы чакаем

па гэты бок плота

мы сочым як дзеці
у шчыліну
за катам каменным
за развалістаю паходкай

"THEY HAVE ME"

Through a small opening
in a concrete fence
I study the shape
of the tyrant's nose

Is it Dzerzhinsky
                    who guards you
in this remote police station?

Armless Dzerzhinsky
with a sharpened nose
signs protocols
fixes your hands at your back
with handcuffs or cable ties
(I cannot tell from behind the fence)

sends you into a white police van
as perfect as a refrigerator?

THEY HAVE ME

now we stand
we wait

on this side of the fence

like children we watch
through an opening
the torturer made of stone

кіроўцы
за бліскучымі шлемамі
касманаўтаў
у святле аранжавай лямпачкі

міліцэйская лямпачка
таксама проста выконвае загад
лямпачка таксама не можа аслухацца
каманды вкл./выкл.
лямпачка прыняла прысягу
на вернасць народу
Рэспублікі Беларусь
і будзе свяціць або не свяціць
як загадае ёй галоўнакамандуючы

лысаваты начальнік
у цемры падобны да чалавека
махае белым сцяжком
з імёнамі нашых родных

отойдите подальше от забора
вы замедляете оформление
вы мешаете работать
их сегодня никто не выпустит
все поедут на Жодино

за плотам
ухвальна шчэрыцца
бюст
носам складаючы
пратаколы

днём я пабачыла
ў шчыліну

the waddle
of a police van driver
the shiny space helmets
in the light of an orange bulb

all a police bulb knows
is to follows orders
the bulb cannot disobey
the bulb took an oath
to serve the people
of the Republic of Belarus
and will shine or not shine
as the commander in chief orders

a police chief
cuts the dark
with a paper flag
with the names of our relatives

the police chief says
move away from the fence
you slow down the process of documentation
you disrupt my work
they aren't going to be released
they will all be transferred further

through the fence
the bust
approvingly smiles

when the daylight came, I saw
it's not Felix Dzerzhinsky

гэта не Фелікс Дзяржынскі
гэта таварыш Фрунзэ

адзін хер

it's comrade Mikhail Frunze

different man
same crime

MY EUROPEAN POEM *

This poem should be written in English.
This poem should be written in German.
This poem should be written in French,
In Swedish, in Spanish, in my adorable Norwegian,
Maybe in Finnish, Danish, and Dutch.
Baltic languages should decide for themselves.
No Belarusian version of the poem,
No Russian version of the poem,
No Ukrainian version of the poem.
The rest are your choice.
This poem should be written in the languages
Of human rights organizations,
Of those multiple concerns expressed
By European politicians.

So
Shall I get used to the thought
That I could be taken to prison
By the men wearing black,
By the men in plain clothes,
By the men with four fat letters
On their fat black backs?
Otherwise, my country.
Won't gain any freedom.
And it could not work anyway,
As usual.

---

* This poem appears, lightly edited, in its original English.

I do not take lightly that I could
Be beaten and ultimately
Found guilty because
(They would say)
I cried antistate slogans like "Freedom!"
Or "Release all political prisoners!"
Though I would not need to cry these words out loud
In order to be arrested or beaten.
I won't have to cry anything,
I won't have to do anything,
Just stand silently, just be.
I know I have to get used to that thought
Just in case, because it's so likely to happen.
(Oh, my! I haven't yet saved those numbers
to contact in case of detention.)

I can't say that in Belarusian,
I can't say that in Russian,
I can't say that in Ukrainian,
Only in English: I am afraid,
Only in German: Ich habe Angst,
Only in Norwegian: Jeg er redd.
That's enough, for other variants,
Please, use Google translate.
The translations should be more
Or less accurate. These are not
Those strange Eastern European languages
With their funny Cyrillic letters.

I'm afraid
Like you would be in my place,
If you lived in a country that is not free

Where they've had the same president
For twenty-seven (!) years. Oh, my god! More than
Two-thirds of my life I've spent
Under the power of a madman
Whom I've never voted for!

Sorry, it's a long poem,
Because it's a long story,
I spent more than two-thirds of my life
Under the power of the man
I've never voted for,
Who harassed and suppressed and killed
(They say).

And when I come to the literary festivals abroad,
And when I speak English
I try to tell the complicated history of my country
(When I am asked)
As if I am another person,
As if I am like all those European poets and writers,
Who do not have to get used to the thought
That they could be arrested and beaten
For the sake of their country's freedom.
As if my ugly history is just a harsh story
That I can easily cut from *The Anthology of
Modern European Short Stories* because
It's too long,
And too dull.

When I tell it in English,
I want to pretend that I am you,
That I don't have that painful experience

Of constant protesting and constant failing,
That nasty feeling of frustration and dismay.
I want to pretend that I have a hope,
Because when I tell it in Belarusian
I realize, we all realize, there is none.

So, forgive me my nagging in a half-broken English,
My Eastern European never-ending complaints,
As having read the books you've read,
I still want to have a hope,
I still believe I have a right to a hope,
That beaten hope that builds its nest
On my roof and sings
In Belarusian
(Not in Russian).

August 5, 2020

Thank you all
for your support.
We do this for you,
and could not do
it without you.

PARTNERS

pixel ||| texel

EMBREY FAMILY FOUNDATION

ALLRED
CAPITAL MANAGEMENT
of
RAYMOND JAMES®

ADDITIONAL DONORS, CONT'D

Mark Haber	Scott & Katy Nimmons
Mary Cline	Sherry Perry
Maynard Thomson	Sydneyann Binion
Michael Reklis	Stephen Harding
Mike Soto	Stephen Williamson
Mokhtar Ramadan	Susan Carp
Nikki & Dennis Gibson	Susan Ernst
Patrick Kukucka	Theater Jones
Patrick Kutcher	Tim Perttula
Rev. Elizabeth & Neil Moseley	Tony Thomson
Richard Meyer	

SUBSCRIBERS

Alan Glazer	Heustis Whiteside	Matt Bucher
Amber Williams	Hillary Richards	Matthew LaBarbera
Angela Schlegel	Jane Gerhard	Melanie Nicholls
Austin Dearborn	Jarratt Willis	Michael Binkley
Carole Hailey	Jennifer Owen	Michael Lighty
Caroline West	Jessica Sirs	Nancy Allen
Courtney Sheedy	John Andrew Margrave	Nancy Keaton
Damon Copeland	John Mitchell	Nicole Yurcaba
Dauphin Ewart	John Tenny	Petra Hendrickson
Donald Morrison	Joseph Rebella	Ryan Todd
Elizabeth Simpson	Josh Rubenoff	Samuel Herrera
Emily Beck	Katarzyna Bartoszynska	Scott Chiddister
Erin Kubatzky	Kenneth McClain	Sian Valvis
Hannah Good	Kyle Trimmer	Sonam Vashi
Heath Dollar	Matt Ammon	Tania Rodriguez

MARIA GABRIELA LLANSOL • *The Geography of Rebels Trilogy: The Book of Communities; The Remaining Life; In the House of July & August* • translated by Audrey Young • PORTUGAL

TEDI LÓPEZ MILLS • *The Book of Explanations* • translated by Robin Myers • MEXICO

PABLO MARTÍN SÁNCHEZ • *The Anarchist Who Shared My Name* • translated by Jeff Diteman • SPAIN

DOROTA MASŁOWSKA • *Honey, I Killed the Cats* • translated by Benjamin Paloff • POLAND

BRICE MATTHIEUSSENT • *Revenge of the Translator* • translated by Emma Ramadan • FRANCE

LINA MERUANE • *Seeing Red* • translated by Megan McDowell • CHILE

ANTONIO MORESCO • *Clandestinity* • translated by Richard Dixon • ITALY

VALÉRIE MRÉJEN • *Black Forest* • translated by Katie Shireen Assef • FRANCE

FISTON MWANZA MUJILA • *Tram 83* • translated by Roland Glasser • *The River in the Belly: Poems* • translated by J. Bret Maney • DEMOCRATIC REPUBLIC OF CONGO

GORAN PETROVIĆ • *At the Lucky Hand, aka The Sixty-Nine Drawers* • translated by Peter Agnone • SERBIA

LUDMILLA PETRUSHEVSKAYA • *The New Adventures of Helen: Magical Tales* • translated by Jane Bugaeva • RUSSIA

ILJA LEONARD PFEIJFFER • *La Superba* • translated by Michele Hutchison • NETHERLANDS

RICARDO PIGLIA • *Target in the Night* • translated by Sergio Waisman • ARGENTINA

SERGIO PITOL • *The Art of Flight* • *The Journey* • *The Magician of Vienna* • *Mephisto's Waltz: Selected Short Stories* • *The Love Parade* • translated by George Henson • MEXICO

JULIE POOLE • *Bright Specimen* • USA

EDUARDO RABASA • *A Zero-Sum Game* • translated by Christina MacSweeney • MEXICO

ZAHIA RAHMANI • *"Muslim": A Novel* • translated by Matt Reeck • FRANCE/ALGERIA

MANON STEFFAN ROS • *The Blue Book of Nebo* • WALES

JUAN RULFO • *The Golden Cockerel & Other Writings* • translated by Douglas J. Weatherford • MEXICO

IGNACIO RUIZ-PÉREZ • *Isles of Firm Ground* • translated by Mike Soto • MEXICO

ETHAN RUTHERFORD • *Farthest South & Other Stories* • USA

TATIANA RYCKMAN • *Ancestry of Objects* • USA

JIM SCHUTZE • *The Accommodation* • USA

OLEG SENTSOV • *Life Went On Anyway* • translated by Uilleam Blacker • UKRAINE

MIKHAIL SHISHKIN • *Calligraphy Lesson: The Collected Stories* • translated by Marian Schwartz, Leo Shtutin, Mariya Bashkatova, Sylvia Maizell • RUSSIA

ÓFEIGUR SIGURÐSSON • *Öræfi: The Wasteland* • translated by Lytton Smith • ICELAND

NOAH SIMBLIST, ed. • *Tania Bruguera: The Francis Effect* • CUBA

DANIEL SIMON, ed. • *Dispatches from the Republic of Letters* • USA

MUSTAFA STITOU • *Two Half Faces* • translated by David Colmer • NETHERLANDS

SOPHIA TERAZAWA • *Winter Phoenix: Testimonies in Verse* • USA

MÄRTA TIKKANEN • *The Love Story of the Century* • translated by Stina Katchadourian • SWEDEN

ROBERT TRAMMELL • *Jack Ruby & the Origins of the Avant-Garde in Dallas & Other Stories* • USA

BENJAMIN VILLEGAS • *ELPASO: A Punk Story* • translated by Jay Noden • SPAIN

S. YARBERRY • *A Boy in the City* • USA

SERHIY ZHADAN • *Voroshilovgrad* • translated by Reilly Costigan-Humes & Isaac Wheeler • UKRAINE

FORTHCOMING FROM DEEP VELLUM